A Picnic of Jokes and Riddles

by VICTORIA GOMEZ

Illustrated by JOEL SCHICK

SCHOLASTIC BOOK SERVICES

New York Toronto London Sydney Auckland Tokyo

ISBN 0-590-31266-9

Text copyright © 1979 by Victoria Gomez. Illustrations copyright © 1979 by Pongid Productions. All rights reserved. This edition is published by Scholastic Book Services, a Division of Scholastic Magazines, Inc., 50 West 44 Street, New York, N.Y. 10036, by arrangement with Lothrop, Lee & Shepard Co., a division of William Morrow & Co., Inc.

12 11 10 9 8 7 6 5 4 3 2 1   10   0 1 2 3 4 5/8

For Doris and Leo Hartman,

my pun-loving parents.

Contents

Monsters and
Other Ghoulish Subjects

What is a monster's favorite sandwich?
Scream *cheese and jelly.*

What does a witch take for a headache?
Broomo-seltzer.

What is Jaws' favorite drink?
Hot **shark**olate.

What kind of arithmetic do soda jerks do best?
Maltiplication.

What do you call a banana that has been stepped on?
A banana splat.

WHEN GHOULS GO FOR A MIDNIGHT CRUISE, WHAT KIND OF BOAT DO THEY USE?

A GRAVE YACHT

How do Indians who have just seen a ghost say hello?
*With haunted **hows**.*

What does a ghost use to go hunting?
*A **boo** and arrow.*

What kind of monsters can make you better when you're sick?
***Gila** monsters.*

When devils get dressed up, what do they wear?
*Silks and **satans***.

What's the best kind of book to read when you have a cold?
***Sinus** fiction*.

Why do vampires walk under ladders?
*Because it's **bat** luck.*

What do you call a giant bell that's covered with hair?
*King **Gong***.

What do you call a soundless bell?
A dead ringer.

Why do bells go broke?
Because of the tolls.

School Daze

Why did the boy's mother make cookies on a rainy day?
*She wanted to see a **son** beam.*

Why did the kid set a piece of chalk on fire?
He wanted a piece of **chalk-lit**.

What is the saddest candy in the world?
Glum *drops*.

How do you get to the dentist?
I take the tooth ferry.

Where do dogs go on vacation?
*To **Collie**fornia.*

What kind of makeup do Louisiana majorettes use?
Baton rouge.

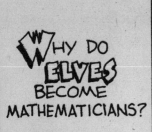

WHY DO **ELVES** BECOME MATHEMATICIANS?

What instrument can almost anyone play?
The shoe horn.

WHAT **TV SHOW** DO PICKLES LIKE BEST?

What subject do runners like best in school?
Jog-graphy.

PUNS DE LEON

What do you call a phony Irish stone?
A sham rock.

Who teaches the Australians to meditate?
*The kan-**gurus**.*

What kind of car did Humpty Dumpty drive?
A **Yolks**wagen.

Where does the sultan keep his car?
In the **garajah**.

What kind of soda do Australian bears drink?
Coca-**koala**.

What did the trader say when he was cheated by a pharaoh?
E-gypt me.

What do you call an Egyptian doctor?
*A **Cairo**-practor.*

Where is most of the money in Egypt kept?
In the banks of the Nile.

What is the definition of lockjaw?
*A **sleep** of the tongue.*

What was King Tut's favorite ride in the amusement park?
*The **Pharaohs** wheel.*

What did the maharajah say when he went into the delicatessen?
Salaam me, please.

SAMURAI WORRIERS

GEE, DO YOU THINK THIS SWORD IS TOO SHARP? OR TOO DULL?

OH, DEAR! SHOULD WE HAVE THE SUKIYAKI OR THE KARATE CHOPS?

WHAT DO YOU CALL A SOLDIER PICKLE?

AN ARMOR-DILLO

EN GARDE, YOU RAPSCALLION!

What kind of places should music lovers avoid?
Vile inns.

Funny Business

Who saw the Brontosaurus enter the restaurant?
The diners saw.

Why should you never tell a secret in a vegetable garden?
*Because of the **beans talk**.*

What's the best article of clothing for a talk-show hostess to wear?
*A **rap**-around skirt.*

WHY DO ALL GOOD HUMOR MEN **LOOK** EXACTLY **ALIKE?**

THEY'RE ICE CREAM CLONES

Why can you never trust train workers?
Because they have loco-motives.

How do woodsmen keep in shape?
*They do their **axercises**.*

Who saw the lumberman cut down the tree?
The chain saw.

What do you call a carpenter who can't find his tools?
*A **saw** loser.*

MY FATHER USED TO BE IN THE ROOFING BUSINESS!

WHY DID HE QUIT?

HIS ROOFS CAVED IN-- SO HE GOT A REPUTATION FOR EAVES-DROPPING!

What kind of dances do opticians go to?
Eye balls.

What kind of rugs do they have at embassies?
Diplo-mats.

Why did the lazy carpenter go to the beauty parlor?
To get his nails filed.

What do you need to build a jail?
*A ton of **brigs**.*

What did the bricklayer say when he lost his cement?
*How **mortar**fying. I'd better throw in the trowel.*

Why do astronauts prefer the hamburgers served in outer space? *Because they're* **meteor**.

Why are perfume makers so rich?
*Because they make a lot of **scents**.*

How does a blacksmith mail a letter?
*In an **anvil**-ope.*

What kind of shoes do lazy bakers wear?
Loaf-ers.

What did one shoelace say to another?
I'm fit to be tied.

Why do astronauts pull out goosefeathers before blasting off?
Because they have to count down.

What kind of bugs bother spacemen?
*Astro-**gnats**.*

What do you call a grandmother sheep?
*A **baa-nanna**.*

Why did the airplane pilot take that black bird along on his flight?
*He needed a **crow**-pilot.*

Why do they call a big ship an ocean liner?
Because it rules the waves.

What do you do when the tide is going out?
Wave good-bye.

Why did the short-haired sailors lose their jobs?
They had a crew-cut.

What do you call a crybaby sailor?
*A **sob** marine.*

Why did the doctor poke holes in his patient's houseboat?
*He was practicing **ark**-upuncture.*

Why was the gambler so happy on the beautiful desert island?
*Because he found a **pair-a-dice**.*

Cops and Robbers

Why did the farmer call the police?
*Because the hen house was riddled with **pullets**.*

WHY DO GANGSTERS JUMP OUT OF AIRPLANES?

TO HAVE A CHUTE OUT!

Why do policemen have the nicest grass in the neighborhood?
*They like **law'n** order.*

WHAT DOES A BURGLAR PLAY WITH IN THE BATHTUB?

A ROBBER DUCK

What did the policeman's wife say when her husband threw up?
*My **cop** runneth over.*

What do policemen eat for dessert?
***Cop**cakes.*

How do secret agents drink their milk?
From a spy glass.

Wild West

What do cowboys put on their pancakes?
*Maple **stirrup***.

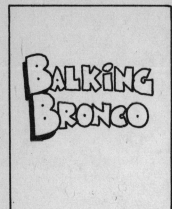

What did the grouchy cow say?
I'm in a bad moo-d.

What kind of horses go out after dark?
Night mares.

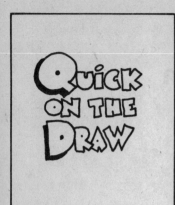

What kind of tears do cowboys cry?
Dude-drops.

Love in Bloom

Why are geological formations like a rare violin?
*Because of the **strata-various.***

BOO-WHOO! BOO-WHOO!

SORRY I'M LATE-- BUT YOU KNOW I GIVE A HOOT ABOUT YOU!

FLUTTERY WILL GET YOU NOWHERE!

BUT DON'T YOU KNOW, I'M FAMOUS! WHY, I AM LISTED IN WHO'S WHOO!

HOW COME?

BECAUSE I'M A KNIGHT OWL!

YOU'RE KIDDING!

ARE YOU CALLING ME A RUSE-TER?

NO-O-O-- BUT WITH ME IT'S OWL OR NOTHING!

I'LL ALWAYS BE AT YOUR BEAK-AND-CALL!

What do kings and queens drink for breakfast?
Royal tea.

Ark Antics

What day of the week did Noah march the animals into the ark?
Twos-day.

How did Noah see where he was going at night?
He used flood lights.

How does a fish weigh itself?
With its scales.

What is the most dangerous place in Alabama for elephants to go?
Tuskaloosa.

What is a monkey's favorite flower?
Chimp-pansies.

What did the duckling say when it saw a parrot?
Quacker want a polly.

What does a dog eat at the movies?
Pup-corn.

What kind of cat has eight legs?
An octo-**puss**

Why did the police stop the chickens' concert?
*They suspected **fowl** play.*

What do you call a group of musical chickens?
*A **squawk**estra.*

WHAT'S THE LATEST **DANCE CRAZE** AT THE DUCK POND DISCO?

Now Appearing....
SATURDAY NIGHT BEAVER

BUMP

THE GOOSE BUMP

What dance did the Pilgrims do?
The Plymouth Rock.

What's the difference between a duck and a spider?
A duck has webbed feet and a spider does web feats.

What do you call a male deer who's crazy about female deer?
A doe-nut.

What is the heaviest soup in the world?
Won-ton soup.

What do you call the winner of an eating contest?
*The **chomp**ion.*

What is a dog's favorite vegetable?
Collie-*flower.*

What is the hardest fruit?
*The pome**granite**.*

What do you call a hamburger bun in a rocking chair?
Rockin' roll.

What kind of soup do they eat at Fort Knox?
Bouillon.

What's a snake's favorite vegetable?
Asp-aragus.

What kind of tile do snakes put on their floors?
Rep-tile.

How do you send a message in the forest?
*By **moss** code.*

What kind of stories do rabbits tell their children?
Cotton tales.

*This book has come to you by **punny express**.*